Colours Of Mind

A Collection of Poems & Sonnets

Pabitra Gayen

BookLeaf Publishing

India | USA | UK

Made with ❤ on the BookLeaf Publishing Platform
www.bookleafpub.in
www.bookleafpub.com

Dedication

This book of poems is lovingly dedicated to my parents, my wife, my son, and my cherished readers, whose love, support, and inspiration have shaped every word within these pages.

.

Preface

White light, when dispersed, reveals a spectrum of colors —just as the mind unfolds in countless shades, each reflecting a distinct emotion, thought, or state of being. The search for these shifting hues is an endless journey of self-discovery.

This collection of poems emerges from that exploration. Each verse captures a fleeting shade of the mind, translating its essence into words. Through joy and sorrow, wonder and reflection, these poems seek to illuminate the invisible.

May they resonate with our own inner colors and awaken new dimensions within.

Acknowledgements

"I offer my heartfelt gratitude to my dear friends, cherished readers, and beloved family, whose constant encouragement breathes life into my words. Through poetry, I uncover the hues of my soul and the vibrant colours of my journey."

1. Kurukshetra and Eternity

Kurukshetra weeps, the war-drums hushed,
Crimson rivers flow where the sun is crushed.
The wind, a mournful dirge for kings now slain,
Whispers secrets only shadows can retain.

Sanjaya stands, his spirit torn and frayed,
Seeking solace where the battlefield is laid.
From the swirling haze, a figure nears,
A sage, time-worn, with eyes like burning spheres.

"Does truth reside in the victor's might?
Is life a candle, flickering in the night,
A fleeting dream, by time's cold breath undone?"
Sanjaya trembles, his voice a whispered plea:
"Has this earth truly drunk such agony?"

The sage's laughter rings, a resonant sound:
"War is but dust on hallowed ground,
A fleeting play of power, soon to cease,
While truth flows silent, a river of peace.

Pandavas, the senses' fleeting sway,
Kauravas, by craving led astray.
Victory's not in vanquished, fallen foes,
But in the soul, where true wisdom grows."

Sanjaya breathes, "Then Krishna, who is He?"
The sage gazes upward, to the boundless sea:
"He is the pole star, guiding through the storm,
The charioteer, keeping the spirit warm,
The fire that melts fear into golden light.
Surrender to His hand, with all your might,
And the path will blaze, clear and bright."

Yet doubt persists, a tendril of smoke:
"Why did Bhishma, Drona, their vows invoke,
And stand with wrong, their honor stained?"
The sage sighs deep, by ages unrestrained:
"Life is a masquerade, a dance of fate,
Childhood Gods fall before time's gate.
Their truths lie buried, beneath the years' decay.
You too will face that reckoning day,
And see – truth is not a blade, nor crown.
All wars are echoes, fading renown."

Sanjaya's voice cracks, a fragile, broken thing:
"And Karna... was his fate a cursed spring?"
A tear glistens in the sage's ancient eye:

"He was desire's captive, beneath a starlit sky,
A noble soul, that stumbled and fell.
Righteousness cloaked in longing's spell,
The burning heart of man, a paradox untold!
But desire's flame, truth's banner won't unfold,
And only ashes rise from life's brief fire,
A cycle of rebirth, fueled by yearning's pyre."

Sanjaya stands, his heart ablaze and raw,
As Kurukshetra greets the twilight's maw.
A thousand questions in the dusk descend,
Leaving behind...
A dusty road, a conch's mournful sigh,
And a vast, silent canvas of the sky,
Where answers aren't etched in cosmic decree,
But felt in the heart, for all eternity.

2. I, Myself.

I am the silent song of infinity,
A riddle spun in time's embrace,
Nameless, formless, yet unbroken,
I rise, I fall—leave not a trace.

Born in the glow of untouched light,
Once ablaze in truth's pure flame,
Yet shadows weave their artful snares,
And I become a fractured name.

At times, I flow—a tranquil stream,
Soft and steady, deep, serene,
Yet when the tempest calls my name,
I shatter, lost in winds unseen.

I dwell within the hush of dawn,
In breath's soft whisper, heartbeat's chime,
Like perfume clings to fallen petals,
I linger in the hands of time.

When humbled, I can touch the sky,
Unfurl my wings on winds so free,
Yet pride consumes my very core,
And turns to ash the soul of me.

Within me stirs an endless strife—
A war of peace, a storm untamed,
Yet still, I seek one lasting truth,
Where I remain, yet none is named.

Beyond all masks, beyond all dreams,
Past fleeting doubts and veils of lie,
I am the fire that never fades,
The light that burns, yet cannot die.

3. Whispers of Eternity

When the doors of the past quietly unfold,
The wandering mind seeks tales untold.
Drifting in the freedom of thought's vast seas,
Words emerge, like a tender breeze.

We cradle them with care divine,
Nurture them with love's soft shine.
Through the heart's window, they take place,
Offering solace, a gentle embrace.

Unveil those windows, let memories stream,
Words hold the essence of life's dream.
Guarded with reverence, pure and true,
They weave life's meaning, old and new.

On the river of life, this fragile boat,
Carries whispers that time once wrote.
Through tears and laughter, in joy or despair,
Whispering words remain, eternal and rare.

4. Home, Sweet Home

Home is the shade of tender care,
A courtyard familiar, love in the air.
A child's laughter, evenings bright,
Sunlit porch in golden light.

Home is a letter, teardrops trace,
A lamp that glows at twilight's grace.
The door that opens, arms that wait,
A heart that beats to welcome fate.

Home is woven in little things,
Joy and sorrow, each one clings.
Warm rice served with love so deep,
A place where hearts their secrets keep.

Home is a pull, a silent plea,
A reason to return, a memory.
Clouds of longing, hands so tight,
A mother's touch, a soft respite.

Home is where our dear ones stay,
A haven where trust lights the way.
No matter where our footsteps roam,
The heart returns to love, to home.

5. Destiny and Kurukshetra

The Kurukshetra war has hushed its cries,
A spectral calm descends where blood-drenched earth
lies.
Crimson sands cradle whispers of the slain,
Echoes of loss—no victor, only pain.

In Hastinapur's dim halls, a queen sits throned,
Draupadi's heart, a labyrinth unstoned.
Her gaze drifts far beyond time's shadowed veil,
Seeking shores where peace might yet prevail.

Krishna arrives, a moonlit silhouette,
Eyes holding cosmos, ancient truths beset.
She trembles,"Tell me—is this justice's guise?
Why does triumph taste of ash, not sunrise?"

He kneels, his voice a river's endless sigh:
"Destiny charts paths no plea can defy.
Vengeance blazed bright, yet shadows linger near—

Does your soul dance lighter, or drown in fear?"

"Duryodhana silenced, Dushasana erased,
But where is the light this darkness replaced?
Karma's roots dig deep through poisoned ground—
Can mercy sprout where wrath once crowned?"

Her voice, a leaf adrift: "Did my wrathful spark,
Weave this ruin, tear the world apart?"
He smiles—"Not at all. You were the flame, not the hand,
A vessel swept by Time's unyielding demand.

The storm you woke was writ in stars long cast,
Yet ask: does healing bloom where fire has passed?"
Her tears carve paths through dust and dried despair—
"Can fate repent? Or merely stand and stare?

The air grows still. A lotus blooms in night,
Its petals cradling dawn's fragile light.
No answer comes—yet in the quietude,
A god's tear falls where mortals weep, pursued.

6. Home Coming(Sonnet-1)

Returning pains the heart so deep,
Yet still, I walk the path once known.
As twilight falls and shadows creep,
My roots still call, my soul is drawn.

Who calls me back—my mother dear?
My father's voice, or soil's embrace?
Does blood remember dreams sincere?
Yet homeward still, I find my place.

The crimson blooms on springtime's chest,
Its burning branches spill their red.
Through pain,love sings,its voice expressed,
As sorrow fades where footsteps tread.

Yet still, I turn to where I'm born,
For crimson flames my soul adorn.

7. Vision (Sonnet-2)

Eyes I have, yet sight eludes,
Veils of illusion cloud the truth.
Deception's snare steals my peace,
In endless circles drifts my youth.

Though outward sight may still prevail,
Can all be known, can all be clear?
Dust has dimmed the mirror within,
The path I seek grows more unclear.

Desires surge like tides, restless,
Greed's wildfire burns unseen,
The heart entangles in love's embrace,
Yet truth dissolves in shadows obscene.

Though my eyes remain open,
Blind I stare, forever broken.

8. Colours of the Spring.
(Sonnet-3)

Upon the streets, the winds of passion rise,
Soft powdered hues now dance upon the air.
With beating drums and love in longing eyes,
Fair Radha stands, her cheeks both bright and rare.

The flute now sings in notes of deep desire,
While crimson hands through golden tresses weave.
The cowherd's touch sets colored dust on fire,
A moment brief, too fleeting to believe.

Now saffron, green, and pink in rapture blend,
As spring's embrace sets hearts and souls alight.
No force can halt the hues that skies extend,
Yet love alone makes every color bright.

If fate should paint my world in shades anew,
Let love be red, let passion burn it true.

9. Eternal Companion.
(Sonnet-4)

Not just a fleeting shade that fades with time,
But one who stays through countless nights and days.
Like vines entwined, in bond so pure, sublime,
With roots that hold where love forever stays.

In humble homes where laughter fills the air,
Through sun and rain, through whispers soft and sweet.
When hunger calls, we soar without a care,
Yet homeward turn, where hearts and hands still meet.

Though tempers rise, we turn aside in vain,
Yet love dissolves like sugar stirred in deep.
"Come to dinner?"—a voice so warm, so plain,
And wounds are healed as bitterness must sleep.

At midnight's touch, our hands in silence blend,
Then drift as one where sky and souls transcend.

10. Not A Poet.(Sonnet-5)

I shall not build grand halls of fleeting dreams,
Nor weave vain words in castles false and bright.
I'll write where sorrow drowns in silent screams,
Where life itself becomes a crushing plight.

I'll write of her, whose birth was marked with shame,
Bound fast in chains she never forged nor chose.
I'll write of him, who rose despite the blame,
And faced the world where every door was closed.

Yet still, a flower blooms in barren clay,
Yet still, its fragrance lingers in the air.
Yet some endure though night obscures the way,
Yet hope persists where none believe it's there.

And still, I write, in words both plain and true,
That men shall say—"He was no poet too!"

11. Silent Grief

Rain falls with a hidden sigh,
Scattering desires across the fields,
Dissolving into the earth—lost, unseen.

Trees bleed from a fleeting touch,
Their sap—a silent wound, unseen pain,
Even the Mimosa trembles, shies away.

A trembling vessel, full yet empty,
Droplets rush to meet the river's song,
Drowning in the vast sea of sorrow.

Once, my heart held an ocean of grief,
Now, both water and sorrow are gone—
Only emptiness echoes within.

12. Holi; A Symphony of colours.

As dawn awakens Holi's cheer,
A burst of hues draws spring near.
Laughter rings through open skies,
As joy and color harmonize.
From rooftops high to lanes below,
Rivers of crimson, sapphire flow.
Yellow, green in clouds arise,
Like a rainbow before our eyes.

With every splash, with every song,
Old sorrows fade, forgotten long.
Hands unite in warm embrace,
Smiles ignite each heart and face.
A festival where love takes flight,
Where shadows melt in golden light.
No fear, no bounds, no past remains,
Just vibrant souls in joyful chains.

So let the colors paint the air,
With friendship, laughter, love to share.
For in this dance, so wild and free,
We weave a world in harmony.

13. True Friendship(Remembering Nirbhaya and her True friend)

That night was dark, cruel, and cold,
Nirbhaya's screams in anguish rolled.
Beside her stood a friend so true,
Alone he fought, though helpless too.

The iron rod struck, his bones gave way,
Yet he stood firm, he chose to stay.
With blood-stained hands,through endless pain,
He fought for her—but fought in vain.

Two shattered lives on the roadside lay,
Torn and broken, left to decay.
No hands reached out, no voice replied,
Yet still, he stood, though all denied.

Through agony deep, through silent cries,
He begged for aid, with tear-filled eyes.
At last, one car—a fleeting chance,
He bore her limp in a desperate stance.

He reached the gates, he called for care,
Though pain still tore his flesh laid bare.
Not once for self did he demand,
Just friendship's vow—his final stand.

Wealth and honor he cast aside,
He walked unknown, yet walked with pride.
None recall his name today,
Yet truer friend—who dares to say?

Now voices rise in protest loud,
Oaths of justice shake the crowd.
But does the world still hear his plea,
Or has his sacrifice faded silently?

14. Forgotten

Like the sun behind a drifting cloud,
Once fierce and bright, now lost in shroud.
They stand in silence, firm yet frail,
Behind each smile, a hidden tale.

Have we seen the light they bear,
The quiet strength, the love, the care?
A soldier masked in sorrow's guise,
A flame that burns where darkness lies.

Father once said, "Speak what's true,"
But truth is heavy, harsh to chew.
Through weary days and nights untold,
Where does trust take root and hold?

The homemaker who counts the years,
With quiet hopes and buried fears,
Steps aside from the bustling street,
To alleys where lost echoes meet.

Once, their laughter filled the air,
Dancing wild, so free, so rare.
Now the city dims their song,
Where nameless faces drift along.

Avoiding glances, heads held low,
Forgotten more than they may know.
Not just by the world they see,
But by the self they used to be.

We sail on rafts of fleeting ease,
Forget the earth, the rustling trees.
Life moves fast, a rushing stream,
We stand ashore, lost in a dream.

And some exist in soulless ways,
Machines that hum through empty days.
Yet buried deep in dust and pain,
A silent song still must remain.

15. Tribute on women's day

Is this just a day of cheer?
Or echoes of pain we refuse to hear?
Dreams extinguished, hopes erased,
A silent cry, a battle faced.

A child with dolls, too young to know,
Crushed beneath a monstrous shadow.
Her laughter lost, her innocence torn,
Now she sleeps where roses mourn.
Today, this day, her name I write,
In silent grief, in burning light.
With all my sorrow, all my pain,
I bow to her in love's refrain.

In a lonely home, an old mother prays,
Her child's name she softly says.
No hands to hold, no voice replies,
Only faith in her weary eyes.
For her today, I send my love,

A sky of peace from high above,
To heal her wounds, to calm her fears,
To gift her rest in golden years.

A woman who built her home with care,
Now walks alone, no husband there.
With three small lives pressed to her chest,
She carries on—she does her best.
She scrubs the floors, she works till late,
Yet love still stands beyond the fate.
For her today, I stand in awe,
She is the fire, the strength, the law.

She who labors in the sun,
Her work, her sweat, for everyone.
Brick by brick, she builds the land,
Yet cooks at dusk with weary hands.
For her today, my heart bows low,
For all she bears, yet none will know.

The woman who dreams, who dares, who flies,
With stars reflecting in her eyes.
Yet whispers wound, sharp and cold,
"Too ambitious," the voices scold.
She stands alone, yet she won't fall,
For dreams still burn beyond the wall.
For her today, I light the skies,

A path of gold where courage lies.

The wife who loves through silent years,
Who hides her wounds,who drowns her tears.
Till truth emerges, raw and cruel—
All her love was not for a real !
Yet still, she rises, she won't despair,
She finds herself in open air.
For her today, my strength, my grace,
A whisper of hope, a warm embrace.

The girl who fights, who stands, who roars,
Who breaks the locks on iron doors.
Who dreams of days where chains are gone,
Where justice sings a fearless song.
For her, I carve my victories bright,
In letters bold, in endless light.

One day will come when none will say,
That women need a single day.
For hand in hand, they'll rise as one,
With strength, with love, with battles won.
No banners raised, no voices plead,
For freedom will be their creed.
And on that day, the world will see,
The dawn of true equality.

16. The Mask of Man(Sonnet-6)

Man smiles, yet poison lingers on his tongue,
His eyes betray the fire of hidden hate.
He mourns another's joy, with praises sung,
While envy plots to twist the hand of fate.

With wealth in hand, his heart is left deprived,
His pride ignites though reason stays afar.
Another's light ensures his own is blind,
His soul consumed beneath ambition's scar.

No cause is needed when he seeks to harm,
For greed delights in wrecking what is pure.
Beneath a painted smile he weaves his charm,
Yet venom waits where kindness seems so sure.

But truth remains, though few may let it show,
Some hearts may shine, while other
s feign the glow.

17. Ingratitude(Sonnet-7)

The hand once raised to lift him from his fall,
Now hurls a stone with ruthless, callous might,
Yet pain nor grief my weary heart enthrall,
He seeks to shroud his shame in endless night.

The one who gives with laughter soft and sweet,
Still marks his gift with chains of secret pride,
A mask of care conceals the dark deceit,
Where selfish power and hollow grace reside.

Ungrateful yet, he stands in haughty guise,
With honeyed words yet treachery within,
Through paths they tread,I walk with watchful eyes,
For careful steps alone the wise shall win.

Yet truth remains,and falsehood fades away,
A grateful heart shall rise in honour's ray.

18. Save Nature(Sonnet-8)

Destroy thou not the earth's unblemished face,
Where birds in song do greet the breaking day.
Let rivers flow with calm, unrushed embrace,
And meadows bloom in light's embrace to stay.

Let golden rays through lofty branches shine,
Where cedars cast their shadows soft and deep.
Let lilies drift upon the silver brine,
Untouched by hands that wake what should not weep.

No reckless step should mar the woodland's grace,
Nor grasping hands defile the verdant plain.
Just watch, just feel, let time its mark replace,
And leave the world untouched, free from disdain.

Though thou depart, the hills shall yet remain,
And nature's voice shall sing in sweet refrain.

19. Stop War(Sonnet-9)

I wait upon the day when guns decay,
When men in olive trade their steel for love.
No cannons roar, no fire lights the way,
But gentle wings bring peace from skies above.

From distant lakes, the birds shall bless the land,
No bombs shall fall where children used to play.
No crimson tides shall stain the golden sand,
But blossoms rise where war once held its sway.

No shattered homes, no cries of dread and fear,
But doves in flight shall grace the open air.
No echoes scream of battles raging near,
Just laughter's song and love beyond compare.

What shall we leave the child who's born today?
A boundless world, where peace shall light the way.

20. Sunita Williams (Sonnet -10)

Not born to yield, nor bound by earth's domain,
A daughter bold, she reached beyond the sky.
Through trials fierce, she rose above the pain,
With fearless heart and vision lifted high.

No chains could hold, no storm could break her flight,
Her strength was forged in knowledge, skill, and fire.
Through realms unknown, she blazed a path of light,
Not bound by fate, nor bent to gods' desire.

Yet mortal still, she fought with will so keen,
Not seeking crowns, nor pleading to the divine.
Her mind, her hands, her daring stood serene,
A force of power, human and sublime.

Let every home a Sunita embrace,
A girl who dares, who leads the race.

21. Inquiry

No minds marvel, no hearts hunger,
Sorrow settles, silence sways.
To question feels faint, forgotten—
A whisper waning in weary winds.
Souls stand still, starved of wonder,
Drifting dim through dust and dusk.

From self to sky, stillness spreads,
No ripples rise, no echoes answer.
Curiosity crumbles, caged in quiet,
The circle of knowing shrinks and shatters,
A flickering flame, a fading fragment,
Where life grows lifeless, lost, and lone.

Yet somewhere still, a spark stirs—
A river restless, rushing, roaring,
Carving currents through crumbling cliffs,
Chasing chances, seeking sight.

For every doubt ,each whispered why,
Fans the fire of fearless flight.

22. My Poetry (Sonnet-11)

My verse, a thirsting lark that longs for light,
A fleeting cry within a boundless land.
It walks through wars that smolder out of sight,
Through kitchen flames where silent grief is spanned.

From World's dark scars to Bengal's woe,
Through shattered doors where helpless voices weep,
Palestine's charred bloom, where dying embers glow,
My lines bear wounds that history dares to keep.

Yet still it burns, no storm can quench its breath,
A marching flame where tyrants forge their might.
It braves the flood, defies the winds of death,
And sings of love when guns surrender fight.

Like mangroves strong through tides of hate and pain,
It walks through fire to bring the light again.

23. Echoes of Defiance

I do not bow to silence's reign,
Though darkness floods the sky again.
The moon is quiet, yet sharp, unshaken,
Its rebel gaze—awake, unbroken.

The ruins whisper, the owls cry,
Their voices tear through midnight's sigh.
A hollow city, mute and bare,
Where even sorrow finds no prayer.

...

Yet I dance with restless winds,
Across a world bends and sighs.
Lightning flickers in my smiles,
As twilight hushes muffled cries.

Like thunder rolling, thoughts take flight,
A thousand voices shatter night.
Truth stands firm—unyielding, bright,
Piercing the dark with fearless light.

Through the haze of fading echoes,
Nightbirds vanish, silence dies.
The world awakes in morning's grace,
To meet the sun with fearless gaze.

24. The Song of the Soul (Sonnet-12)

My sorrow hums in notes of deep despair,
Like Tilak Kamod's melancholic strain.
Sindhu-bhairabi's echoes linger in the air,
While Jayjayanti sings of joy and pain.

A silent grief adorns my sacred hall,
Like drowning boats that drift in fleeting time.
Love's pulse is lost within its rise and fall,
A lotus floats—her grace untouched, sublime.

At times, my heart will dance in bliss untold,
Yet then, it steals and strips all joys away.
In ruins framed, the painted tales unfold,
Where Darbari Kanara weeps and sways.

Had I but learned to weave my cries in tune,
Then sorrow's song would release, and bloom.

25. Desire Rekindled

I yearn to paint a sky so vast,
Yet words retreat, elusive, outcast.
My mind protests, "The hour is late,"
And so, I linger, bound by fate.

But Desire murmurs, soft yet clear,
"Embrace the unknown, cast aside fear.
Observe the world, let rhythms guide,
Words will awaken, rising with the tide."

Let the sky remain untouched, unspoken,
Its boundless beauty a sacred token.
Let spring's breath stir my soul's ember,
A fire that burns, a light to remember.

For,in the silence, truth takes flight,
A quiet blaze that banishes night.
Let desire's flame forever burn,
And peace in every heart return.

26. Humanity

A starving child, a pleading gaze,
Knows no color, creed, or race.
Rama, Rahim, Buddha, Christ—
All the same in love's embrace.

Where work prevails, let faith reside,
No walls of hatred, none divide.
Man above all—name or nation,
Love alone—the true salvation.

Let kindness bloom, let hatred cease,
Let hearts unite in boundless peace.
No chains of religion, no marks remain,
Only love, in every one's vein.

Still, we fight, still, we part,
Will love not mend each broken heart?
Will dawn not rise, with hands entwine,
Where hate dissolves, hope can shine?

Eid , Christmas or Puja's light,
May all songs of love be bright.
No swords, no blood, no cries of war,
Only more peace forever.

I dream a world, so vast, so free,
Where love alone is destiny.
No walls remain, no chains divide,
Only humanity as our guide.

27. The Call

Can you quench the earth's deep thirst,
Restore the life it once had nursed?
Can you bring light to sightless eyes,
And stir new dawns in silent skies?

We seek a voice, steadfast and true,
To end the dark, to birth the new—
Not life to lose, but pain to fade,
Let hope arise, let night evade.

Can words ignite a blazing fire,
To break the chains, to lift us higher?
Truth alone can wake the deep,
Revive lost faith, let shadows weep.

Can you rebuild a land betrayed,
Where trust decays, where dreams have swayed?
Will your voice stand bold and high,
Defying wrong, upholding right?

If you can, then rise and stand,
Let echoes sweep across the land.
If truth still burns within your soul,
The world will sing of justice's goal.

28. The Kiss

A kiss, sudden, unbidden,
Fell from his lips like a spark—
Fleeting, reckless, vanishing,
Yet burning into memory.
Her eyes had held something familiar,
Like a road once walked,
Like a moment half-remembered,
Just beyond his reach.
Then, nothing.
No trace, no return.
Only the weight of her breath,
Pressed into his skin like a secret.
His wife leans in,
Her touch steady, certain.
He gives her all—
But when she lifts her lips,
He turns away.
"Not this," he thinks.
"This is hers."

For in that single kiss,
He carries a world—
One he can never return to,
One that never truly left.

29. The Wanderer

In civilization's earliest stride,
On untrodden paths, mankind did glide.
The solemn heart sought unknown bliss,
By rivers deep or forests' abyss.

By vast, unending streams they stayed,
Or mountain caves their roots were laid.
Life was struggle, a tireless fight,
Dreams of green lands, bathed in light.

From Nile to Rome, from Greece's reign,
From Sindhu's flow to kingdoms' domain,
Empires flourished, thrones rose high,
Yet the earth grew burdened, its voice a sigh.

Now mankind stumbles, borders ensnare,
In caste, in creed, in faith's despair.
A shrinking world, with doors shut tight—
Is there no path to endless light?

Yet man still moves, through lands unknown,
By will, by force, by fate's undertone.
Are laws for man, or man for laws?
Can rules suppress life's boundless cause?

Forever a wanderer, man must be,
To cross all bounds and journey free.
Through time and space, he'll always strive,
To seek a home where dreams survive.

30. The Cloud

Wandering alone, I met a cloud, suddenly!
It asked, "Do you know me? Can you recognize me?
I drenched you once, by the field's edge, unexpectedly."

"You soaked me then,
With endless showers again and again.
You filled my heart, my soul entire,
And sang of joy, igniting desire."

In silent whispers, untold tales flow,
Revealing truths only the heart can know.
It drifted high in the boundless skies,
Leaving behind longing and sighs.

You brought me joy,
You carried pain.
In life's pendulum swing,
Time washes away every stain.

Yet, as the wheels of life revolve,
At twilight's edge, I hope to resolve—
Perhaps I'll meet that cloud once more,
Awakening echoes from my soul's core.

I asked the cloud,
"Do you enjoy drifting free?"
The cloud replied,
"Drifting is what defines me."

But suddenly, what do I see?
The dark cloud's heart split apart,
Pouring tears from a heavy heart.

The wistful cloud, so eager to roam,
Now vanished, lost, far from home.
Leaving memories to linger deep,
In the quiet sea of my soul to keep.

31. Even If Not

Even if dreams bring no delight,
Be my sorrow, stay in sight.
With my pain, I'll carve my way,
Let my grief not drift away.

Even if songs of joy don't play,
Be my ache, don't fade away.
With each wound, my soul will grow,
Let my heart with longing glow.

Even if stars don't light the skies,
Be my spring, where fire lies.
Let your flames burn fierce and high,
Be the thorn I can't deny.

Even if the sky turns black,
Be the clouds that never lack.
Pierce the dark with golden hue,
Be the sunbeam breaking through.

32. Rain

The rain called softly, beckoning me,
"What is it that you wish to see?"
I smiled and said, "I ask for naught,
The joy you bring is all I've sought."

"I've poured my soul in endless streams,
Yet why do you drift in hollow dreams?"
"In your touch, the world feels new,
No gift is richer than drops of you."

"I rise from nothing, fall, and fade,
Mingling with the mist I've made.
Yet the fleeting days between,
Shine in memories, pure, pristine."

The heavens wept in silver song,
And life awoke, renewed and strong.
With hope reborn in golden light,
I'll weave a home in love's delight.

Let love rain down, let love remain,
Let hearts be cleansed in tender rain.
Within your touch, so soft, so true,
Let love be born in drops of you.

33. Agnodice:A Flame in the Dark
(The struggle of Athens' First Woman Physician)

In Athens' halls where wisdom grew,
No woman's voice, no healer knew.
The temple doors were shut so tight,
For men alone to claim the right.

Yet one dared dream—defying fate,
She cut her hair, she masked her state.
In secret halls, by lantern's glow,
She learned the arts no girl could know.

A mother's cry rang through the street,
Her pain too fierce, her hope too weak.
"No man shall touch me!"— came her plea,
Agnodice knelt in secrecy.

With healing hands, so kind, so sure,
She eased the pain none dared endure.
The news spread fast—her name revered,
While jealous men grew cold with fear.

"Deceiver! Fraud!"— their voices swelled,
"A woman cannot heal!" they yelled.
They dragged her to the court of stone,
And sentenced her to die alone.

But voices rose—a mighty tide,
Women stood fierce, stood side by side.
"If she must die, then so shall we!"
The judges quailed—her chains broke free.

And thus was carved in history's scroll,
A woman's fight, a victor's role.
When gates are locked and paths turn stark,
Agnodice's flame still lights the dark.

34. Rhythm Zero: The Human Mask

At first, the room was soft with petals' fall,
A silent saint - Maria, still for all.
Some fixed her hair, some kissed her cheek so fair,
While flowers crowned her brow with tender care.

But clocks don't lie - as mocking hours crept,
The hands that blessed grew violent as they swept.
Rose stems became the whips that tore her dress,
Each tick unveiled more brutal nakedness.

They carved her skin with blades they'd brought to bless,
Spit in her mouth with drunken cruelty's caress.
One pressed cold steel against her pulsing throat -
The crowd became a single snarling goat.

When end came shivering in the pallid light,
No eye could meet her gaze - all dropped from sight.....

35. When I am Nowhere

Spare not a tear—let it freely flow,
When I am gone, where echoes go.
Seek me not in empty air,
But in your heart—I'll be there.

Hold no sorrow, no grief for me,
You cannot hate me—this I see.
Though time may pull your heart away,
Closer than ever, I shall stay.

Close your eyes—feel me near,
Touch me not, I fade too clear.
Send me forth with joy, not pain,
Let me go like a song in rain.